Tito and the Bridge Brigade
A Collection of Short Stories

DAVID GONZALEZ

RAINART BOOKS FOR
YOUNG READERS

ISBN-13: 9798631390959

Cover design by: Art Painter

Library of Congress Control Number: 2018675309

Printed in the United States of America

DEDICATION

To all my childhood friends, we were the village.
D.G.

*I could not bear a life
with everything perfect.*

- Jimmy Santiago Baca

CONTENTS

TITO AND THE BRIDGE BRIGADE

"As long as he can bring the dog." You had to hand it to Mom; she knew how to make deals. Mom was on the phone with Uncle Milo about me coming to visit my cousin out in the country for the summer and insisted that Tito was part of the package. "He's a sweet pup. Doesn't poop in the house and doesn't bark, much." That comma there, between 'bark' and 'much,' that's important because, even though Tito was mostly quiet, when he sensed that something was wrong, he would bark like crazy, and wouldn't stop howling till whatever it was stopped. Like, once, when I walked him around the block, he started barking at an empty alleyway between two apartment buildings, but at what? There was nothing there. Well, nothing I could see. Then a woman came out, screaming that her two-year-old was missing. Tito was barking, the woman was crying—and I didn't know what to do. Tito pulled so hard on the leash that he broke free, ran down the alley, got to the end, looked back at me, and barked some more. I ran down to Tito and saw the "missing kid" happily playing with a doll in the parking lot behind the building. Tito saved the day. He was like that, with a superhero's sense of danger, and how could you not love a cuddly, cute, long-haired cocker spaniel with those kinds of mad skills? I adored him, so when Uncle Milo said it was fine to bring Tito, I jumped for joy.

Milo was the youngest of Grandma's siblings, and the wildest. Grandma was the second oldest of eleven kids, so by the time Milo was born, Great-grandma Elenora was so distracted, so exhausted, or just so fed up raising a pack of kids that she let Milo figure it out by himself. His older brothers and sisters did what they could, but Milo was born a wild child, and nothing they did made much of a difference. They lived in a tiny town with dirt roads and no stoplights on the edge of a lush forest; let's say *jungle,* in Puerto Rico, and Milo made that jungle his playground.

When he was ten he built a fort of giant palm branches, climbed coconut trees to get the juiciest *cocos,* and raided the neighbor's farms to snag vegetables and berries. He could imitate most of the bird songs he heard, and with a shovel and his bare hands he made a little canal from the stream to his hideout so that he could have his own supply of fresh drinking water. He was like a Puerto Rican Mogli, or like the guy who was raised by wolves, except that he pretty much raised himself. When the family left Puerto Rico and moved to New York City, Milo never felt as if he fit in. As soon as he could afford it, he bought property upstate, where he could raise animals, plant vegetables, and roam the woods again.

Milo's son, Dana, was one of my favorite cousins. We were exactly the same age, listened to the same rock music, and loved to take our bikes for long rides, so spending the whole summer together was going to be fantastic; plus, Tito would be there too.

Uncle Milo never stood still. Maybe you've heard about 'restless leg syndrome,' a rather odd condition where someone can't control the jumpy jiggling of their legs. Maybe you even know someone who has it. Well, Milo had 'restless life syndrome'—he never sat down. There was always a new project that Dana and I had to help him with: put a new fence around the chicken coop, shovel that ten-foot dirt pile into the pigpen, scoop the muck out of the pond. And we did it because, well, we had to, and because Milo promised us a huge surprise at the end of the summer.

Usually, I wouldn't fall for this kind of suspicious plan; I mean, who would? It seemed like a lame way to get us to work, but then again, it was summer, and we had plenty of time to play with Tito and to ride our bikes, and what if maybe, just maybe, the surprise was actually awesome? We put a hundred miles on our bikes that summer, and Tito loved being away from the city. He trotted along beside us, chased squirrels, rolled in the mud, swam in the creek, and once, even caught a little snake. And the chickens got a new fence, the pigs got their dirt pile, the pond got clean, and then, two weeks before I had to go back to the city, Uncle Milo sprang his big surprise. "Guys, here it is. Okay . . . drum roll . . . I bought an island! And you guys are going to help me build a bridge to it."

What? Who buys an island? How big is it? Where? And how the heck are we, who know nothing about building anything, going to build a bridge? Isn't that a seriously complicated thing to do? Don't you need special training, special tools, special skills? But Milo was so confident he could do it, and so certain that we were going to love it, that we played along and signed up for the project.

So the next day, Dana and I, along with Tito, piled into the back of Milo's rusty green pickup truck and drove to the lumberyard. Milo told the men there that he was building a bridge and needed a lot of wood. The lumberyard guys rolled their eyes, as if to say, "This guy is nuts, but, whatever." I could see that Uncle Milo didn't care what they thought; he knew what he was doing, these guys were just dumb. We loaded the pickup with a ton of wood, literally a ton, two thousand pounds of boards and planks, and fifty pounds of special nails that wouldn't rust if they were exposed to water. Milo also bought Dana and me our own hammers and leather holsters with a metal loop on them to hold the hammer onto our belts. Now it was getting cool. When we finally got to the property, I saw that Milo had invited his friends Oscar and Jimbo, and their kids, to help, so altogether there were about twelve people on the bridge-building brigade, plus Tito, of course.

We hiked down a long, steep grassy hill and came to the place where the bridge was going to be built. Milo told us the bridge needed to be five feet high and thirty feet long to get to the island on the other side of the creek. But it had been raining for a week and the current was so high and fast that Tito immediately started barking. As soon as I saw the situation, I looked at Dana and we both knew this was ridiculous; there was no way we were going to build a bridge over that rushing water. Milo said this was *no problemo,* easy-peasy, and started to tell us what to do: "You hold this, you bang that, you get more wood from the truck, you tie a rope around that tree . . ." I did as I was told, but the whole time I got more and more worried, and Tito would not stop barking; this really freaked him out. Milo got mad at Tito and told me to go back and lock him in the truck. I brought Tito all the way up to the truck and was careful to leave the windows wide open so he wouldn't get too hot. But the whole time he was in the truck, he kept on barking as if his life depended on it.

When I got back, tempers were heating up. Oscar was telling Milo that this plan was not going to work, and Milo told Oscar that he could leave if he didn't trust him, and so he did; he grabbed his two kids and left.

That made nine of us. Dana was standing in the creek up to his waist, struggling against the rushing water to hold an eight-foot board straight, while Milo was on a ladder trying to hammer another board onto it. A sudden rush knocked Dana off balance. He bumped into the ladder, causing Milo to fall into the water and lose his hammer in the current, and cursing Dana for being such "a stupid idiot." Yeah, there was that side of Milo too. Ever notice that people who are unbalanced in one direction tend to be unbalanced in the opposite direction too? Milo was "can do, can do, can do" all the time, except that when he "couldn't do," it made him lose his mind, lose his temper, and lose control, and that is exactly what was happening. Dana apologized and went back to holding the board, Milo grabbed the hammer out of my holster, got back on the ladder, took one swing, missed, and went flying into the water again. And now he was really mad, but instead of taking a break to get himself together, he yelled at Dana again. And he yelled so loudly that Jimbo's four-year-old daughter, Emma, started crying and tried to run away, but she slipped on the mud and tumbled into the water. Jimbo dove in to get her, but the current was way too strong, and Emma was so small that it carried her into the deepest, fastest part. We ran along the bank looking for a way to grab her, but it was impossible. Jimbo was swimming as fast as he could, but the current swept her away faster than any of us could swim or run.

And then, out of nowhere, Tito bolted down the steep riverbank, took a flying leap into the water just in front of Emma, grabbed Emma's T-shirt in between his teeth, and pulled her to the shore. Jimbo wrapped his arms around Emma, I wrapped my arms around Tito, Dana patted his head, and Milo sat in the muddy water with his head in his hands, saying over and over, "I'm sorry, I'm sorry, I'm sorry."

Big surprise, the bridge never got built. Milo sold the property and invested the money in a taco truck. Dana liked tacos but refused to work in the truck and started playing the guitar instead. And as for Tito? Me and that wonder-dog were besties for a long, long time.

PYRAMID POWER

Everybody has advice for a kid whose dad has disappeared, especially Mom's boyfriends. Carmelo, the waiter from the cruise ship, tells me to learn how to cook, that cooking relaxes the mind. "Make spaghetti sauce," he says. Ernesto, the physical therapist, puts it like this, "Go jogging. It'll get you into a happy zone." Sergio, the banker's version is simply, dumbly, "Forget about your father, he's a jerk, life is short, get out there and just have fun." And my cousin José, a man of few words, says, "Judo," and by that he means that the martial art of judo is the only way I am ever going to become a man. The way he says it, with such confidence, with such certainty, makes me believe he might be right, but then again, he is my cousin José, probably my least favorite relative.

I call him Cousin José because technically he is, but he is old enough to be my uncle. He has a stocky build, looks like a box; his chest is almost square; and he works out with weights so much that his arms stick out from his sides, and his neck, well, he has no neck, just meaty shoulders and a head. His head is a box too and his huge square glasses don't help. But what is most boxy about him is his brain, the way he thinks, and the way he talks—when he speaks to me I feel that I'm inside a tight, dark, crowded box, with sharp corners. José talks in one-word grunts. He eats a plate of Abuela's incredibly delicious arroz con gandules; all he manages to mumble with a full mouth is "good." Or if someone cuts him off on the highway, he'll say *"pendejo."* These single words are how he communicates with the world. So when he says "judo," I know not to ask why, or how, or where. José figures his manly responsibility to me is done with that one simple word. Judo.

José hardly ever smiles, and if he does, it is a snarky "yeah-right" kind of put-down smile designed to make you feel dumb. Amazingly, he is a grownup who never learned how to have a conversation. A conversation is that wonderful thing that humans do where we listen, then talk, listen some more, then talk some more, like that; everyone giving and taking about the same amount. It's a basic skill, like learning to write your name, like brushing your teeth before bed, like learning the times tables. Everyone learns how to have a conversation; it is simply something you have to learn to do, it's how the world works. Except José, who must have cut kindergarten the day they were teaching conversation. José either blurts out his one-word comments or dry bits of advice, or he doesn't say anything, and when he is quiet, you know that he is angry. Oh, he'll say he is bored, but he is angry.

I am surrounded by women: Mom, Abuela Lupe, Titi Ida, Titi Carmen, Titi Dima. I love them *and* I am really curious about how to be a man. I know I am a male, but being male is not the same as being a man, so when José tells me that judo is the way to become a man, I take it to heart.

And there it is, taped to the wall at San Antonio's afterschool center, a big, bright poster, JUDO CLASS STARTING NEXT WEDNESDAY. San Antonio's Church gym is where I go to play pool and basketball until Mom gets back from working downtown as a bilingual secretary. The poster has row after row of kids in white baggy pajamas, with colored belts; white, yellow, red, green, black. The kids in the picture look intense, like they are ready to jump off the page and kick my butt. Their snarling faces look like they're yelling a war chant directly at me. I can't picture myself in one of those rows screaming like that, but still, if I wanted to be a man . . .

According to Wikipedia, judo is *a martial art whose most prominent feature is its competitive element, where the objective is to either throw or take down an opponent to the ground, immobilize or otherwise subdue an opponent with a pin, or force an opponent to submit with a joint lock or a choke.*

So the words that freak me out in this Wikipedia article are *take down, immobilize, joint lock, and choke.* None, absolutely none, of these words are things that I like, want to be a part of, or even want to hear. But if José is right, if judo is the way to be a man, then bring on the *joint locks*, whatever the heck that means.

The very short diary of a judo dodo.

Week one:

I've got butterflies in my stomach, I've got zero skill, I'm too skinny, I'm too weak, I'm uncoordinated, twenty push-ups? I'm lucky if I can do five. I watch the more experienced kids fake-fight each other; kicking, grabbing, throwing, pounding, flipping, pinning, squeezing, and basically beating each other into dust. I'm *thinking,* "If this is fake fighting, then what will real fighting be like?"

The teacher, a hyper-loud, super-fit guy, comes up to me and says, "Okay, we start with the basic position, the stance; legs apart, fists at your hips, punch out right, yell 'HO!' punch out left, yell 'HO!' repeat . . . repeat . . . repeat . . . good."

He said "good" to *me*, whew, through week one.

Week two:

Warm up by running around the church gym ten times, then fifty jumping jacks, then twenty push-ups, (I squeeze out six), basic position, HO! punches, and then grabs. Grabs are when you grab your opponent by their shirt. There I am, face to face with a kid I've never met before. He goes to grab me, I trip on my judo pajamas and tumble backwards onto the floor. I get up and apologize. He tries again. This time he grabs my shirt and I don't fall, but I do stumble a little. Next time he tries to grab me, I fall again, and apologize again. My turn. I grab his shirt; he doesn't fall. Three times in a row he just stands there, like you're supposed to. Then the teacher announces a "fun way to close the night—The Human Pyramid!" Whoopee. I *do not* want to do this, but all the other boys seem to think the human pyramid is the most exciting thing in the world. Six boys line up on the floor on their hands and knees, then five boys (including me) kneel on top of them, then four boys on top of us, then three, then two, till a final kid is on top. Ta-da, a human pyramid.

My back is killing me, I don't feel strong enough, I'm embarrassed for not wanting to be there but being there, and then the whole stupid pyramid crashes down. Some kid's elbow hits the side of my head really hard. It hurts like crazy, but I don't say anything because everyone else is having so much fun. And then the teacher yells "Again!" The boys scream with joy, and I want to run away but don't. With my aching head, I take my position on the second level. Again the pyramid gets higher and higher, and when the top boy is finally in place, the teacher yells, "*Now stay there. Don't move. Stay. Don't talk, don't laugh, don't do anything except be a pyramid.*" My back is sore, I'm even more embarrassed, and then I feel terror. *What if I can't stand it anymore? What if I'm the weak link? What if I am responsible for the pyramid crashing down?* I hold on. I try to ignore my aching back. I try to control my arms when they start to shake. I am sweating hard and breathing hard, my eyes are shut tight, my teeth are clenched, the side of my head is hurting, I am concentrating with all my might but can't stop the shaking in my arms; it gets worse and worse. I feel terrified.

"Don't move. Stay there," the teacher shouts. And then he starts chanting "Pyramid Power, Pyramid Power, Pyramid Power," and all the boys join in. 'Pyramid Power, Pyramid Power, Pyramid Power,' louder and louder, and the shaking in my arms is getting out of control. "Pyramid Power!" and then my legs start shaking too, then my whole body, and then my worst fear comes true. My arms give out and the whole pyramid collapses. This time I take a knee in the chest, but still the other boys laugh and the teacher gives high fives all around. I pretend that I am fine. I pretend that it wasn't my fault. I pretend that I am having fun, and when the teacher says, "One more time!" I tell him that I have to pee, and run into the boys' room, get into a stall, lock it, and sit on the toilet holding my aching head, wishing I were anywhere but here. I stay in the stall till I hear the pyramid pile crash one more time, at which point the teacher dismisses the judo class.

The next time I see José, he asks how the judo was coming along. I lied and said it was good, but I never went back. It wasn't the teacher's fault, it wasn't José's fault, it wasn't my fault. It just wasn't my thing, and neither was cooking or jogging, and just forgetting about my missing dad, as if that were even possible, that was never going to work. I knew I had to figure out my own way to grow up, my own way to become a man. Whatever that means.

ACTION

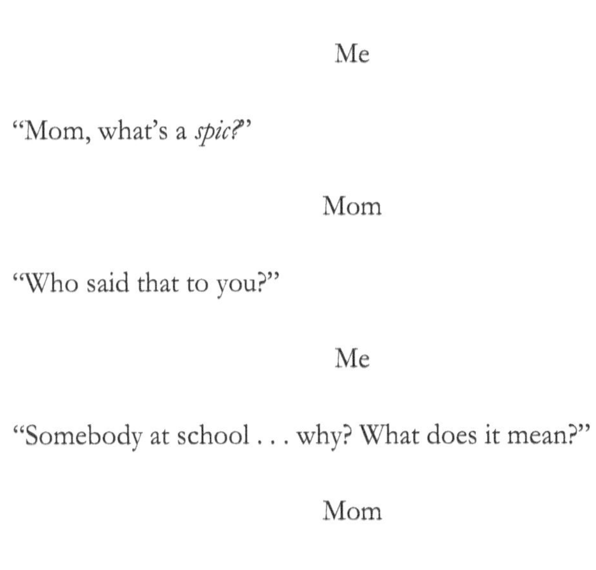

Me

"Mom, what's a *spic?*"

Mom

"Who said that to you?"

Me

"Somebody at school . . . why? What does it mean?"

Mom

"It means whoever said that ugly word to you is a jerk. Now forget about it and go do your homework."

Me

"But, Ma . . ."

Mom

"But nothing. *Vete a tu cuarto a estudiar y olvídese de ese idiota.*"

I knew when Mom switched into Spanish it was serious. It could be serious-happy, like when she would kiss me goodnight and say *"mi angelito,"* or serious-anger, and this time it was definitely that one; she was mad that someone had called me a spic. So I did as I was told; I went to my room to do my homework, but I could not get that word *spic* out of my head, and I definitely could not forget the *idiota* who said it to me.

Not that I would ever call John Dubensky an idiot to his face. That would be suicide. His nickname was Maddog, known by everyone as the biggest bully in the school. Every morning, without fail, he would show up with three big letters written in black Sharpie on his upper arm— *M.D.X.* We knew the *M* was for MAD, we knew the *D* was for DOG, but that *X* was a mystery. What did it mean? *X* like *I'm eXtremely dangerous,* or *X* like *I'm going to eXecute you,* or maybe *X* as in love and kisses xoxoxoxo. That homemade tattoo scared the crap out of me. I'd heard that once, in art class, he took scissors and cut four inches off the ponytail of the girl who sat in front of him. Then there was the time that he said he was going to punch a teacher in the face. Then the famous incident when Maddog climbed on top of a statue in the park and yelled "FU!" to the cop who was trying to get him down. All I could say was thank goodness Maddog wasn't in my class and thank goodness I only had to see him in the hallways, at lunchtime, or in the schoolyard—all of which were places where I could avoid direct contact with him.

So imagine my surprise on the first day of middle school when Maddog showed up in my sixth-grade homeroom. My heart sank, my stomach turned, and my head spun. *This has got to be a mistake. Maybe I can transfer into a different classroom. Maybe he'll magically self-destruct into powdery dust and be blown away.*

No such luck. Maddog took a seat in the last row of the classroom, directly behind me. The teacher took attendance, and when she called out "John Dubensky," he grunted, "Yeah." Then she began laying out the ground rules: the attendance sheets are collected every afternoon at blah, blah, blah, lateness reports will be sent in at blah, blah, blah, parent-teacher meetings happen every blah, blah, blah . . . I couldn't pay attention to a single word she said because my brain was focused on the Maddog problem.

I've heard that when people get really sick, like when they get diagnosed with a fatal disease, it is normal for them to pretend it isn't real, like if they pretend hard enough the sickness will go away. Of course it doesn't, but that kind of hoping seems to be hard-wired into people, and I had it too. "This has *got* to be a mistake. This *cannot* be happening. Isn't he too dumb to be in sixth grade? He should have been left back. Isn't there a special school for criminals? *What the hell!*" My only relief was at least we didn't have gym or lunch together.

Four different elementary schools sent kids to MS 127, my new gigantic middle school about a mile from my house, so there were lots of strangers in my new homeroom, but there were also a bunch of kids I recognized from my old school; not that they were my friends, but at least they were kind of familiar, and there was Carlito and my cousin Margarita.

His full name was Carlos Miguel Perez Hernandez, but everyone called him Carlito, A) because his father was named Carlos, so at home he was 'little Carlos,' aka Carlito, and B) because he was really short and skinny; he looked like he belonged in fourth grade, not sixth. He wore big glasses that slid down his nose, and he had a slight speech impediment where he sometimes pronounced *S* like *SH,* so "shoes" became "shuth" and "guys" turned into "guyth," as in "Guyth, gimme my shuth." Add to this the fact that Carlito was super-smart. He read all the time and was placed in a special class for math tutoring, where he worked on tenth-grade problems. Carlito played the violin with the Bronx Symphony Orchestra, and sometimes even beat Mrs. Diaz, the science teacher, in chess. The dude was a freaking genius. He was my friend, and even though he sucked at sports, talked funny, and was the size of a peanut, and even though I was no macho tool myself, I tried my best to look out for Carlito.

My cousin's full name was Margarita Anna Rosario Karlsson. She was born exactly one week before me and loved to say that she was my big cousin. Margarita wasn't short for anything; she was called Margarita because our great-great-grandmother was Margarita. Family folklore said that this Margarita had a special gift, that she knew things that no one else knew or could know. For instance, she could find someone's lost keys by closing her eyes and breathing deeply, concentrating, and *Boom!* she would see their exact location. And she claimed she could see the future, like the time she predicted a massive hurricane, even though the sky over Puerto Rico that day was as blue as could be. So, of course, when my cousin Margarita was born, everybody thought that if they named her after Great-great-grandma, she might inherit some of her magic.

Margarita's mom and my mom were sisters and we basically grew up together. Slideshow, please! Here we are at two months old, sleeping in the same crib; here we are at six months old, wearing the same onesies; now we're ten months, going out on the town in side-by-side strollers; and here we are at fourteen months, kissing. What? Ew! She was my cousin! Whatever. We were babies.

Margarita was definitely not a baby anymore, she was actually ahead-of-the-pack developed. She had always been tall for her age, and during the summer between fifth and sixth grades, she really shot up. We knew the reason for her being so tall was her dad, Lars Karlsson. Yep, my Puerto Rican *titi*, Ida, married a blond, six-foot-four guy named Lars. When the teacher called out her name, "Margarita Anna Rosario Karlsson," she said, "Present, and please call me *Rita.*"

Rita? Whatever. It was the first day of middle school and she wanted a fresh start.

Okay, so in this mystery/adventure, I've got a villain (Maddog), a person-to-be-saved (Carlito), an ify ally (Rita), and myself. Now all I had to do was wait for the action to start.

Action!

When the homeroom period bell rang, everyone rushed the door. I was near the back of the pack, trying to squeeze through to get to music class, when I felt someone pressed up against me. I was about to say, "Hey! Gimme some space," when I saw that it was Maddog. I swallowed my words and instead quietly muttered, "Uh, hey, Maddog," trying to sound cool. Maddog said nothing …zero, zip, *nada.* It was as if I hadn't spoken at all, as if that moment in time had never happened, as if I didn't exist. Which was fine with me; I was willing to pretend that I didn't exist if it meant that Maddog didn't notice me.

Luckily, he didn't follow Carlito and me toward the music room but headed down toward the gym, the same place where Margar—where Rita—was going. And that was the first time I felt protective of her; a little red warning light started flashing in my brain.

Later, on the walk home, she said that Maddog didn't bother her but did give her a look. "What kind of look?" I asked. "Like the look the wolf gives Little Red Riding Hood, like 'I'm smiling, but I'm actually going to kill you' kind of look?"

Rita said, "No, it was more like an 'I'm pretending to be tough, but I'm really sweet on the inside' kind of look."

"Ugh!" I said. "I freaking hate that guy. He's lying to you with that look. He was in my school. He's the worst bully in the world."

Rita, who seemed to be in a daydream, just said, "He's cute."

"No, no, *no*! He is definitely not cute. Cute is dimples and a lollipop. He is a monster," I yelled.

"No, actually, he is cute. I know cute from not cute, and that boy is most definitely cute," Rita said.

"Fine, cute," I said. "If cute means terrifying."

"Well, he doesn't terrify me, and I don't judge people by what others say about them."

This was a typical thing for her to say. She was like a human version of one of those Character Education posters that you see on the wall next to the guidance counselor's office. Rita could, and would, actually say things like, "There is no *I* in TEAMWORK," "Caring is thinking with your heart," "Respect—you've got to give it to get it." And she would say these things in public!—to her friends, to total strangers! When she said these things I wanted to cover my ears and pretend that I didn't know her. I tried to ignore this less-than-wonderful quirk of hers, but I had my limits, and she had just crossed them.

"No, Margarita, no!" I yelled at her. "Maddog is not cute, he is not caring, he does not know the word *respect,* and he is not a team player. Didn't you see his tattoo? Didn't you see the *X?*"

"Sure, I did. *X,* as in love and kisses," she said.

"Nooooo. *X* as in *execution,* as in death!"

In a calm voice, Rita said, "You have lost your mind. Calm down, nothing happened, and, okay, I will keep an eye on John. Nothing bad is going to happen."

I muttered, "Oh, so now he's *John?*"

"He is to me," Rita said with a tone of pride.

"Whatever," I hissed.

"What did you say?" Rita asked.

"I said that your new best friend Maddog called me a spic yesterday."

"Bull," Rita said.

"He did. Ask him. I dare you," I spat back.

"I will," she said.

"Good."

Long pause.

"What is a spic, anyway?" I asked, embarrassed that I didn't know.

She breathed a long heavy breath through her nose, her lips were pinched up, her eyes were intense. "*Spic* is a horrible word used to insult us Latinx people. It makes me so freaking mad."

The next morning, Carlito was nose-deep into a book while the homeroom teacher took attendance. Maddog shuffled in late, walked by Carlito, and purposely bumped him so the book fell on the floor. I couldn't believe that he was picking on Carlito. That was way low. I looked at Carlito as if to say "are you all right?" He shrugged his shoulders and tilted his head, with a look that said "this happens all the time. I'm used to it."

I don't know where it came from; I was scared, but I looked at Maddog and weakly said, "Leave Carlito alone."

Maddog shot me a look like the twin barrels of a shotgun. "Oh, so the spic is tough."

I froze.

"He is, and so am I," Rita snapped at Maddog, then she walked right up to him and said, "Apologize to Carlito, and for saying that nasty word to my cousin. *Now!*"

"He's your cousin?" Maddog said, shocked. I could see the anger that had been in his face melt into a look of sadness, as if his dreams had suddenly gone poof.

"Say it!" Rita insisted.

Then I said it. "Say it."

Then even Carlito said it. "Say it."

Maddog was dazed for a few moments. He looked at the three of us and spat out, "FU to all of you!" then ran out of the classroom.

The next day, he didn't show up to school, which was a huge relief to me.

"Doesn't surprise me," Rita said, then dropped one of her Character Ed sayings, "Inside every bully there is someone waiting to be loved."

"Oh, c'mon, Rita, really?" I said impatiently. "Maddog is waiting to be loved? You've got to be kidding. What he is waiting for is a chance to punch me in the face."

But when he finally did show up at school, Maddog was, well, he was different. He took his seat in the back of the classroom. When the teacher said his name, he said, "Here," like the rest of us. When we piled out for our first class of the day, he stayed behind, and when I looked back, I saw that he was walking toward the gym. The flashing red light went off in my brain and I wondered if Rita would be okay."

That whole day I was scared of what Maddog would do to me if he got me alone. I stayed close to the other kids and didn't go anywhere by myself. At the end of the day, back in homeroom, I found a note on my desk, written in black Sharpie.

"Sorry for what I called you. John, aka *MDX*."

I looked over at Carlito and he had the same note.

When I turned to look for Maddog, his desk was empty.

As we walked home, Rita told me that Maddog said he was sorry to her too. She said she told him that she accepted his apology, and then asked him what the *X* stood for.

"You're never going to believe it," she said.

"You mean, it's not *eXecute?*" I asked.

"Nope. That *X* stands for *exists,*" she said. "As in, *Mad Dog eXists.*"

"Yeah, right," I muttered.

Rita said, "I think he is really, really sad on the inside, so he tattoos *MDX* on his arm to remind himself he is okay, that he is here."

"You figured all this out on the way to gym class?" I asked.

"Yup, and on the way back," she said. "And at lunch."

"You had lunch together? Are you crazy?" I yelled. "Don't trust him!"

"Don't worry, I've got this," she said.

And so from time to time Rita would sit with Maddog at lunch, right under the poster that said *Treat Others The Way You Want To Be Treated,* the one that none of us paid attention to, but I've got to say that Marga—oops, I mean Rita—did.

Maybe it was just that Maddog grew up, maybe it was Rita's determination, or maybe it was Great-great-grandma's magic. Whatever it was worked because Maddog never bothered Carlito or me ever again.

REYNALDO'S DAD

There are two worlds. In one world, kids know what kids know. In the other world, adults know what kids *don't* know, not to say that grownups know everything that kids know; mostly, they don't. They know what it's like to be a kid, but they definitely do not know a kid's secrets. And kids don't know what adults know, but they do know that adults have secrets too. These two worlds live side by side, they interact, they are both part of the "universe-of-human-experience," and they are very separate. That's a good thing because kids need privacy, and even though kids want to know everything in the adult world, they also sort of don't. But every once in a while these worlds smash into each other.

My cousin Reynaldo had super-curly red hair and freckles. Not so strange except, yes, it was. For a Puerto Rican to have red hair was like a Chinese person with an Afro—you just don't see too many. The mystery of that coloring was solved many years later with DNA testing, but that's another story for another time. The fact of Reynaldo's freckles, the fact that his dad could never be mentioned, the fact that my *titi*, Carmen, was bonkers, and the fact that they were coming to live with us made me think, "Yep, the two worlds are definitely going to collide."

Even though our big family all lived in the five boroughs of New York City, Reynaldo's mom had taken him as far away from there as possible. After fifth grade, Titi Carmen packed up her rickety old Chevy, plopped Reynaldo in the seat next to her, and proceeded to drive for five days across the entire country to Los Angeles. Why? Answer: mystery. Why did they come back? Answer: mystery. How long were they staying? Answer: mystery. So, with all these mysteries to be solved, we waited on the stoop in front of the apartment for them to arrive.

Okay, whoa. First of all, Reynaldo was driving. He'd gotten his learner's permit in California, and because Titi Carmen's bonkers-ness sometimes showed up as paranoia, she was afraid to handle the car in the city and made Reynaldo drive. I mean, driving on the straight highway is intense, but driving in the city takes some serious skill. So when they pulled up with Reynaldo behind the wheel, we were impressed. Plus, when he got out of the car, he was a giant; well, if you count his hair. Reynaldo had shot up to five foot ten and had grown his hair out into a four-inch puffy red Afro that bobbed up and down with every step he took. When he walked toward me, what I saw was an enormous red-headed, freckle-faced . . . stranger. And what made it even weirder was how shy he was. The giants in my dreams were in-your-face vicious monsters, but Reynaldo seemed so unbelievably gentle that, quickly, another mystery was added to the pile: *Who is this guy?*

We had fixed up the basement as a guest room for them, and after some of Abuela's arroz con pollo and plátanos, the worlds separated, the grownups stayed around the kitchen table, and I took Reynaldo across the street to the park. There's something about shy people that makes me wonder what they keep inside; for instance, is their shyness covering something they are afraid to talk about, or are they shy because that's just how they are? I never can tell, so with Reynaldo I started asking questions.

How was school in California?

Decent.

Did you see movie stars in Los Angeles?

Nope.

Do you surf?

Tried it. Sucked at it.

Why did you go there in the first place? Long silence.

Why'd you come back? Long silence.

Looooong silence.

I said, "Sorry, man, we don't have to talk about it."

Reynaldo said, "Answer to your first question: my dad. Answer to your second question: my dad."

And then his story came pouring out.

It turns out that Titi Carmen took Reynaldo to California because his dad was drinking a bottle of whiskey every single day. At first he was what they call a "social drinker"; you know, just at parties, but then he started drinking alone in the house at night. The hangovers messed with his sleep so he couldn't get up in the morning. Reynaldo's dad lost his job when Reynaldo was in third grade, and just kept on drinking, thinking that if he drowned his problems in whiskey, they would go away. Then he lost his . . . um, I guess, kindness. He'd yell at Titi Carmen, and then one day he hit her, and that's when they left.

Reynaldo hadn't seen or talked to his dad in six years. He never got a letter, not a call, not a birthday card, *nada,* nothing, and the only bits he heard about his dad from the grownup world were that he was still drinking, still out of work, and sometimes even sleeping on the street.

"And why did we come back?" Reynaldo went on. "Is 'cause now my dad is really sick and I wanted to see him again before he . . ."

That's when Reynaldo began to cry. There we were on a park bench, in my neighborhood, in public. There I was with this freckle-faced giant, this stranger, and he was crying, and crying hard. It was as if he'd been waiting for a chance to let it all out. I don't know why he chose me; maybe it was just the right time, or, who knows. The fact was that Reynaldo was sad, and scared, and mad, all mixed together.

In between his tears, Reynaldo said, "That jerk couldn't get his life together to take care of me. He freakin' hit my mom. He ruined everything. And now he is going to die and I don't know what to do. Do I tell him how mad I am, do I tell him all the things he could have done to be a better dad, do I make him regret his life? Or do I pretend that I'm okay? Do I pretend that me and my mom going to Los Angeles was the best thing for all of us, just to help make his last days a little easier? Or do I actually find a real way to forgive him. What am I supposed to do?"

Long silence.

I put my arm around Reynaldo's shoulder.

Long silence.

I had no idea what to say.

Long silence.

Loooooooong silence. Then Reynaldo quietly said, "Thanks, man. I just needed to tell someone. I'll figure it out. C'mon, let's shoot some hoops."

Reynaldo shared his secret world. He told me tough things about the adult world I didn't know, and somewhere in that difficult truth-telling the two worlds combined, and my long-lost cousin Reynaldo and I became friends.

BLACKOUT

"Se fue la luz!" Abuela called out to me in the alley where I was playing punchball with Dio and the guys. Punchball is like kickball, but where you punch instead of kick. Carlito was on third, I was at bat. "Gimme a break! I'm about to slam a homerun and bring Carlito in, can't it wait?" I shouted back at her. *"¿Tu estas loco?"* she yelled back. And that was that; the game stopped and I went inside to turn the power back on. Everyone in the family had their responsibilities, and one of mine was resetting the circuit breakers. Uncle Milo had taught me how to do it, and ever since then, I was the one to grab the flashlight, go down to the basement, go inside the dusty utility closet, open the circuit breaker box, search for the flipped breaker, flip it to the other side, and ta-da! Light!

Sometimes the lights went out in the daytime, which wasn't so bad unless Abuela was in the middle of sewing or watching her favorite telenovela.

If they went out at night, the house would go completely dark, and Tito would bark as if a stranger had suddenly appeared in the living room, or like the sun had suddenly stopped shining. If it happened in the middle of the night, we would wake up and the clock would show the exact minute the power went out, like 3:31 a.m.—then I would have to reset the breakers, and the clocks, before breakfast.

I liked to pretend that I had a superpower where I could send electricity through my fingers into the breakers to bring light back into the house. I have to admit that I felt, um, what's the word—special? No, important, no, um, useful! Yeah, that's it. I felt useful when I got the electricity to come back on. It just felt good.

"¡Gracias!" Abuela said. "Come back en *diez minutos."*

When I got back outside, the game was over. Dio had to go home for dinner and the rest of the guys were trading baseball cards. I wasn't into it, so I just went back inside for some of Abuela's tasty *carne guisada.* After I stuffed myself with her beef stew, we sat down on the couch to watch TV. About an hour later, Tito was asleep on my lap and the power went out again, and Abuela again yelled, *"Se fue la luz."* I went back to the kitchen for the flashlight, thinking that I must have done it wrong earlier. That's when I noticed that Señor Garcia's house across the alley was dark too. Our kitchen windows faced each other and it would have been normal for their kitchen light to be on, but it wasn't. I looked out the window down to the apartment building behind our house and not a single light was on. Lots of people were yelling *"Se fue la luz!"* Tito started barking like a maniac.

When I told Abuela what was going on, she went out the front door to the street. I followed right behind her. The whole block was dark; all the houses, all the street lamps. People were piling out of their buildings, everyone was talking a mile a minute, asking questions, trying to figure out what was happening. Tito was hopping up and down, yapping like crazy. Señor Garcia turned on his battery-powered radio and all the neighbors huddled around it as he searched the scratchy airwaves for news. Finally, a voice said, "A massive electrical jolt has knocked out the lights for the entire city. Power company officials cannot say how long the situation will last."

"Caramba," Abuela said. *"Se fue la luz* in de whole city!"

I couldn't get Tito to stop barking. He was totally freaking out.

What I imagined we needed was a Godzilla-sized dude with a flashlight as big as a lighthouse, flipping a breaker the size of a car.

It was a hot and sticky summer night, and with the power out, the air conditioners and fans didn't work, but luckily Chucho did. Every night for every summer since I could remember, we would wait to hear the salsa music from Chucho's brightly lit ice-cream truck as he drove down the block. He'd park right in front of our building, slide up the window, perform a dance move, and with his booming voice, say, "I eh-scream, you eh-scream," and we'd all yell back, "We all eh-scream for I eh-scream!" The combination of his ear-to-ear smile, the music that blared from the speaker on top of the truck, and the colorful ice-cream posters plastered all over it made Chucho's visit the brightest time of any summer night.

Everyone surrounded Chucho's truck and Abuela asked him what he knew. *"Se fue la luz,"* he said. A loud chorus of kids shouted, *"We know!"* *"¿Que mas sabes?"* Abuela wanted to know what else he knew. Chucho told us that every house on his entire route was dark. *"El hospital tambien?"* Abuela asked nervously, wondering if the hospital had power, because her cousin Juana was on a breathing machine there. *"Si, tambien, pero tienen un generador y todo esta bien,"* Chucho said, giving us the good news that the hospital had a generator for these situations. Abuela sighed, *"Gracias a Dios,"* and went to sit on the stoop. I ordered a Creamsicle, my favorite—smooth vanilla ice cream surrounded by icy orange sherbet—and sat down with Abuela. After Chucho and his truck disappeared down the street, we settled in for a round of family gossip. Abuela loved to talk about the family, but her specialty was talking about the Rosado family down the block, who always seemed to be in the middle of one crisis or another.

Abuela pretended that everything was all right, but even with all the familiar stories and gossip, it was kind of spooky. What was a "massive electrical jolt?" How *exactly* did the power go out? Was there an attack or something? When would the power come back? *Will* it come back? All Abuela could say was *"Todo va a salir bien."* Her chilled-out 'everything is going to be all right' attitude didn't help. Mom had left for work early that morning and we hadn't heard from her since the power went out, so Abuela went in to see if maybe, by some miracle, the phone was working again. I sat on the front steps pretending that I was cool with the situation, but I wasn't.

It was then that I noticed someone walking very slowly up the block toward our house. Since the street lights were out, I couldn't tell who it was, but whoever it was walked so slowly that it was kind of creepy. I squinted my eyes, trying to figure out if I recognized the guy, and finally saw that he had a long white cane with a red tip that he swiped side to side as he walked.

I watched as he tapped his walking stick, getting closer to our stoop with every step. When he was right in front of me, Tito started barking, and with a heavy American accent, the man said, *"¿Buenas noches. Agua por favor?"*

"What?" I asked.

"Sorry. I thought you spoke Spanish," he said.

"I do, but . . ."

"Must be my terrible accent. I'd sure love a glass of water, if you can spare it."

Just then, Abuela appeared at the front door." *¿Con quien hablas?"* she asked angrily, wanting to know whom I was speaking to.

"Me llamo Bill. Solo quiero un vaso de agua," the stranger said in his basic Spanish.

"Mijito, un vaso de agua," Abuela said. When I came back with the glass of water, she was talking to the guy in her less-than-perfect English.

"Weh ju leeb?" she asked him.

"My apartment is about twenty blocks from here," he answered. "The bus isn't running, so I'm walking."

"Das a lon weh," Abuela said. "Especially since ju no see."

"It's okay. I like the exercise. Plus, I got to meet you!" he said, flirting with her.

"Are ju hongri? I can gib ju som carne guisada." She pointed to me, then to the kitchen, then to the guy. A minute later, I arrived with a plate of food.

"Delicioso," the stranger said.

"So, ju ehspeak EhSpaneech?" she said.

"Un poco," he said. *"Me llamo Bill."*

"Me llamo Guadalupe." Abuela told him, "My grandson is Davicito."

For an endless hour, Abuela told Bill stories about growing up on a small farm in Puerto Rico, and just when he finally had a chance to tell a story about being in the army, and how bombs were falling all around him, the phone rang. I went inside. It was Mom. She was on the subway when the power went out and had been stuck there for two hours. When she finally got out, she went to her girlfriend's house and found a phone that worked. I told her about Bill.

"What?" she said. "Do not talk to strangers. Put your *abuela* on the line!"

I said, "Ma, it's okay. He's a good person. He just needed a glass of water. He's just about to tell an amazing story."

"Put. Your. Abuela. On. The. Phone."

I went back outside and begged Bill to finish his war story, but we could hear Mom and Abuela arguing on the phone. Bill said, "I think it's time for me to go."

I asked him if he'd be okay getting home.

"Yeah, sure. The lights never went out for me, y'know," he said with a little laugh. "I mean, I can't see light the way you can, but I sure can hear it; like, your *abuela*'s voice shines with sweetness, and I'd say you are lit up with curiosity. Get me?"

I thought about it, then said, "Yep, I do."

"Please say *adios* to your grandma." Bill said it like *ah-dee-os,* corny, but funny, then waved his white and red cane, tapped it on the ground, and slowly disappeared down the block.

We used candles to light the house that night, and instead of watching TV like we always did, Abuela told me stories, even one about the time when her pet donkey ate her father's wallet, *with cash inside.* The power came back on the next morning, Mom came home, and things went back to normal. I always wondered what happened to Bill that day when the bombs came down, and how it was for him to see into people the way he did.

CHEMBO'S WORLD

The playground and basketball court were right outside Chembo's door. He could literally walk straight out of his apartment building and get into a game, and since I lived two blocks away, that is where I played too. Chembo lived in the city housing projects, and even though his building was really crappy, and even though they had elevators that got stuck a lot, the fact that the playground was right there was a major plus. We became friends as toddlers, playing for hours on the slides, swings, seesaw, and monkey bars. Chembo's family had come from Mexico when Chembo was a baby. Señor Chapa washed dishes in a restaurant, while Señora Chapa took care of an old lady in the building. We hung out together so much that people called us *Las Chanclas*, "The Slippers," because we were always a pair, always together. At parties we put on *The Chanclas Show*, where Chembo, who was really funny, played "the wild and crazy guy," while I was the "straight man" who pretended not to know what was happening.

Chembo had the amazing, but annoying, talent of always having to tell the truth. He couldn't say even the tiniest little lie. Once, we got back to his apartment forty-five minutes late for dinner and he actually told his mama that we had been throwing snowballs at the elevated subway cars. I mean, he could have said we helped a guy with a flat tire, or we shoveled out a pregnant lady's car, or *anything*, but no, Chembo always told the truth. Though this was definitely a hassle sometimes, mostly it made me trust him.

Simply put, we were best friends, forever.

Chembo's bedroom was completely, and I mean *totally,* covered in tin foil. Well, except the floor, it was fake wood, but all four walls and the whole ceiling were shiny silver. He'd used a staple gun and tape to put it up . . . roll after roll of the stuff, so that when you went inside, it was like a house of mirrors, freaky but cool. And when he turned on his little spinning multicolored disco ball, the whole place glittered as if you were traveling through space at the speed of light. For the final touch, he would play some weird music on his ultra-bass sound system so that the world outside faded away and "Chembo's World" became our reality.

Chembo had worked on his room the way a scientist works on finding the solution to a mysterious problem: by trial and error. The beginning experiments didn't work; the plastic wrap sagged, and wax paper was just boring. The tin-foil solution solved it, but not right away. For his first try, Chembo worked really hard to keep it super-smooth, with hardly any wrinkles anywhere. It was cool, but he realized the little parts where there actually were wrinkles made the light bounce around more. So he took it all down, crunched it up, and re-hung the tin foil with just the right amount of wrinkles.

Then there was the question of where to put the disco ball so it would have the biggest impact. He started in the middle of the ceiling. It was okay, but when he tried it in the corner, he liked how the moving lights stretched out and got longer in weird ways. He was serious about making "Chembo's World." His bossy big brother, Roberto, had left for college and finally he had his own room. "Chembo's World" would be his private palace, a place where he would be in charge.

And so "Chembo's World" became our hangout, because, let's face it, it was way cooler than my room. After school and on weekends we'd talk, listen to music, and do our homework together, which could be challenging when rainbow lights are zooming all around. When Roberto came home for college vacations, Chembo got to keep the tin foil, but the disco ball was shut down because it gave Roberto a headache, which made him cranky, which made him a pain in the butt.

But not always. Sometimes Roberto was awesome and would take us to weird places and do stuff that we didn't usually get to do. One time he said that Chembo and I could come with him to a New Year's party at the house of one of his college friends. It wasn't every day that we got to go downtown, especially to the fancy part of town, *especially* to a college-kid party. To be honest, we both felt a little scared and embarrassed to be going. I mean, besides Roberto, we didn't know anyone, and they were all like seven years older than us. Also, it felt kind of dumb to be there as someone's little brother and his sidekick. But Roberto told us it would be fun, and that he'd treat us to a frappuccino on the way. So I put on the new clothes I had gotten for Christmas, went to their house, and hung out in "Chembo's World" till it was time to go to the party.

It was a long, loud, crowded subway ride from where we lived to the Upper East Side. But it was the holidays and I could tell that people were pretty happy, so I settled into my seat and talked with Chembo about the party.

Me

"Okay, so let's make a deal. We stay close to Roberto, right?"

Chembo

"Def."

(High five)

Me

"We stick together."

Chembo

"Def."

(High five)

Me

"We do not drink, smoke, or do anything stupid."

Chembo

"Def, def, def."

(Three high fives)

Why I ordered a frozen frappuccino, I don't know. What I *do* know is that a brain-freeze on an already freezing January night is not anything I would wish on anybody. Slurping my way through the windy city streets, my head stinging, I kind of wished I were back in my warm, comfy house. Roberto steered us block after block through the neighborhood where the party was going to be. There were no bodegas, no cheap wig stores, no cuchifrito restaurants. Instead, there were jewelry stores, fancy clothes shops, and super-expensive restaurants. We were def not in the hood anymore. Finally we stopped outside a three-story brownstone building with Christmas decorations around the windows and in the little garden in front.

"What floor is their apartment on?" I asked.

Roberto said, "Dude, Jason's family lives in the whole building."

I'd never been in a house like that before. The ceilings were ten feet high, shiny wooden stairs went up and down, fancy carpets lined the floors, weird squiggly paintings covered the walls, and a humongous chandelier with a million glass beads hung over the biggest dining table I'd ever seen. The place was packed with people.

"Yo, Jason!" Roberto cried out.

Jason, wearing white bunny ears, turned, ran over, and gave Roberto a bear hug.

"You must be Roberto's little bro," he said, looking at me.

I said, "Me friend, he" (pointing at Chembo) "bro."

Then Jason grabbed the two of us and hugged us too.

"So glad you little dudes could come," he said. "The sodas are in the fridge next to the beer, the bathroom is upstairs, and the game room is downstairs. Have fun. C'mon Roberto, I have a surprise for you."

Roberto followed Jason upstairs and we went to look out the window to the garden; yes, they had their own big garden behind the house. And even though it was winter, and even though it was really cold, there were a bunch of people outside.

"Let's explore!" I said.

"Def."

The first stop was the kitchen. To get to the fridge, we had to squeeze between a couple that was making out and a guy who was staring up at the light with half-closed eyes, rocking from side to side. Chembo looked at me and rolled his eyes, as if to say, "Weird, whatever . . ."

With sodas in hand, the next stop was the game room. Whoa. This place made our afterschool center look like a junkyard. The lights were low, the music was loud. There was a wooden pool table, a Ping Pong table, an old-school pinball machine, an arcade-worthy video racing game, a foosball table, and a big TV/Xbox with a black leather couch.

All the games were taken except Ping Pong, so we found two paddles and started hitting the ball back and forth. Chembo was a beginner, but I had played a lot at the afterschool center. Two minutes after we started, two college guys came over and said, "Let's play doubles." Without asking, they grabbed paddles.

"Nah, you guys can have the table," I said.

"No, c'mon, doubles is fun, and hey, if you guys don't want to, we'll just wait and watch till you're done," they said.

So now it was either play doubles or have them watch us play. This was the definition of that old saying "Stuck between a rock and a hard place." We were stuck, with no easy way out.

Chembo saved the day and said, "OK, but I suck at this, so we have to make it even. One of you guys has to be my partner."

"Done!"

These guys were way better than us. Basically, we became spectators as they whacked the ball back and forth, trying to stay out of their way. Luckily, they quit after five minutes, and as they were leaving, they asked if we wanted to go outside with them.

"Def," Chembo said.

In my head I was thinking, "What? No!" but out of my mouth popped, "Yeah, cool."

So we headed upstairs, and with each step, that voice in my head got louder . . . *this is weird; don't go outside with these guys.*

I poked Chembo in the ribs and gave him a look like, *what are we doing?*

Chembo whispered, "C'mon, live a little."

I whispered back, "No."

"Your choice," he said, as he slipped out the back door to the garden.

There were about ten people outside, smoking and drinking beer, and that same couple was making out again.

I watched from inside as Chembo followed the guys to a group of people who were passing around a cigarette. *Flashing-Red-Light!*

I pulled my collar up and went outside, grabbed Chembo by the elbow, and said, "*What the heck?*"

"What?" he said.

I hissed back at him, "1. We promised to stick together. 2. Where is Roberto? 3. This is stupid!"

"C'mon, dude, it's a party, chill out," he said as he turned and walked back to the group.

"I'm getting Roberto." I went back inside the house but didn't see Roberto in the living room or the game room so guessed he was upstairs somewhere. It felt good to get away from all the strangers and loud noise. When I reached the second floor I saw that a door was open at the end of a long hallway; I heard voices and people were laughing, so I walked right in.

Big mistake.

Well, I found Roberto all right. He was cuddled up on a bed with two other guys. None of them had their shirts on. Roberto was facing away from the door. I tried to do a quick spin and get out before they could see me, but no luck.

One of them said, "C'mere, dude." It was Jason, talking in a sloppy, drunken voice.

And then I heard Roberto's voice say, "Yeah, there's room for more in the cuddle puddle."

"Uh, no thanks," I said, and turned and left.

"Damn!" I heard Roberto say.

As I went down the stairs he chased behind me, buttoning up his shirt. "Sorry, dude . . . I didn't know it was you. Um, don't tell Chembo what just happened, okay? He'll tell Mama and Papa, and if they find out I'm gay it'll be real *mierda* in the house. I mean, I will definitely tell them one day, but not now, not yet, I'm not ready. I can't deal with them freaking out. Okay? Promise?"

I thought about it for a second, gave a tiny nod. "I want to go home" was all I could say.

"*No problemo*. Where's Chembo?"

"Outside, smoking."

"Oh, hell no!" Roberto said, then grabbed his jacket from the closet, stormed outside, put Chembo into a headlock, and dragged him back in.

"What the . . ." Chembo yelled.

Roberto demanded, "Did you . . ."

Before he could finish his question, Chembo said, "No! When they passed it to me, I shook my head. I didn't."

Roberto took Chembo's face in his two hands and stared right into his eyes. "Don't lie to me."

"I. Don't. Lie." Chembo said each word as if it were a hammer pounding on a piece of concrete.

"Can we just go home?" I asked.

On the walk to the subway, Chembo asked Roberto where he had been while we were playing Ping Pong. Roberto shot me a look, then said, "I was talking to Jason up in his room."

That subway ride home lasted an eternity.

I carried the weight of Roberto's lie like a backpack full of bricks till he went back to college. A couple of days after he left, Chembo and I were listening to music in "Chembo's World," the lights spinning all around, and I told him what I had seen upstairs at Jason's party and how Roberto made me promise not to tell him.

Chembo was quiet for a long time. "Yeah, I pretty much guessed he was gay," he finally said.

"You can't tell your parents. Roberto has to do it when he's ready, not you," I said. Even if they ask you straight up, you absolutely cannot tell them."

"But I can't lie," he said.

"Yes. You. Can," I said. "Your parents would freak out."

Long pause. Then, in a quiet voice, he said, "Yep, they would."

Long pause.

"Rock and a hard place," he said.

We sat there in silence for a long time, the two of us traveling through space at the speed of light in "Chembo's World."

DADDY LONG-LEGS

Like me, Dio, Juanito, and Ivan knew Alvaro's weak spot and, as a testament to our tribal honor, didn't let the goons in on it. Who knows what they'd do to initiate a kid into the troop. That's what they call a bunch of apes too, a troop, yeah, those apes, the ones with alpha males, the ones who fight to protect their territory, the ones who pound their chests and howl. About 30 boys had come into the Boy Scouts from different neighborhoods, so the five of us, The Pushkees, a name taken from a store we liked on the Lower East Side called The Pushcart, stuck together. Sure, we'd sing "A Hundred Bottles of Beer" with everybody else when we hiked, and sure, we'd cooperate in the cooperation games, but when it came down to it, we were our own little troop-in-a-troop, and nobody was going to spill the beans on our weak spots. Not that we'd made a pact or anything; it was just a fact, the way of the world, *you don't reveal the soft spot.* Mine was being alone, long story there, but let's just say that being alone freaked me out—my monsters stay away when I've got company, but when they see that I'm alone, they creep out to mess with me. *What about at night,* you might be thinking. Yep, they visit my dreams. A lot.

We all knew each other's soft spot. Juanito absolutely could not be criticized or else he'd blow up, at himself, actually punch his own head. Dio could not *not* be liked—if his amazing charm and smile didn't work on someone, if they ignored him, or even worse, if they rejected him, he'd be crushed; not right away in front of them, but as soon as they were gone, Dio would sink into a black hole. And Ivan, he knew everything there was to know about sports: the players, the plays, the odds, but because of a back surgery he'd had when he was four years old, he couldn't actually play. He sucked at running, was terrified of falling, and his throwing arm was, well, let's say it was underdeveloped. If teams were being chosen, he would say he wasn't into it or he had to go home, or some other obviously lame excuse.

And Alvaro's was spiders, especially daddy long-legs. Even though Mr. Perez, our science teacher, had taught us a lot about arachnids, the harmless ones like daddy long-legs and the poisonous ones like tarantulas and scorpions, Alvaro grouped them all together into the category of terror. Luckily, we didn't see many spiders in the city, and he had no problem with cockroaches, but when we went to Ten Mile River Boy Scout Camp that summer, there were tons. I guess it wasn't too hard for the older kids to figure out Alvaro's weak spot. He was constantly on the lookout for spiders in the bunk, on the trail, in his shoes, everywhere. It was like me and my imaginary monsters, only spiders are very real, and very much at home in the woods; you couldn't *not* see them. As much as Alvaro hated spiders, he wouldn't kill them. If he saw one he'd freak out, and then run as far away as he could. The Pushkees swept the bunk at night, shook out his sleeping bag, and basically added eight more eyeballs to his nerve-racking vigilance.

For whatever reason, my initiation was pretty harmless, though frustrating. The older Scouts sent me on wild goose chases all the way down a lonely forest path to the camp office for the famously non-existent *left-handed-skyhook*. When I returned empty-handed, they sent me back, almost two miles, to get an *under-seat-outhouse-brush*, and when that was a bust, I went to fetch a *particle-wave accelerator*. Of course, being new, and of course, believing that I needed their approval, I did these ridiculous tasks until they'd had enough fun at my expense. But they had other plans for Alvaro.

One night, after lights-out, when we were all sound asleep, it must've been around midnight, four of the older Scouts snuck into our cabin, woke us up, and told us to stay quiet, that they had an amazing thing to show us. Being the newest kids we followed them single file away from the campsite, past Señor Santiago, the Scout leader's cabin, deep into the woods. Then they grabbed Alvaro and pinned him on the ground, telling us to keep quiet, or else. One kid sat on Alvaro's legs, one on his right arm, one on his left. The other kid pulled Alvaro's T-shirt up to his neck, stood over him, took out a jar and poured a stream of honey onto Alvaro's bare chest, and smeared it all around. Then he took out an old coffee can, peeled off the plastic lid, grabbed a daddy long-legs out of the can, and held it by one leg as it squirmed and wriggled. The other kids had flashlights so that Alvaro could see him dangle it over his eyes, and then he dropped it onto the honey so that it got stuck to Alvaro's chest. Then he dropped another one, and another one. Alvaro screamed, cursed, and cried. We tried to stop them, but they warned us that we'd get the same treatment if we didn't shut up, or if we squealed to Señor Santiago. They dropped nine daddy long-legs onto Alvaro—it didn't last long, maybe two minutes, but it was torture, and torture-time isn't the same as regular time; every second lasts an hour, and the memory lasts forever.

After they dropped the last spider on him, they ran back, laughing, to the campsite. We picked the spiders off Alvaro, wiped the honey from his chest, hugged him, and cursed those kids for being such damn jerks.

I told Señor Santiago what they had done, but he didn't punish them, and instead said, "Boys will be boys." I thought, "Hey, I'm a boy, but I would never do that to another kid." Alvaro went home the next day, but I had to stay for another week, always looking over my shoulder to see if they were coming for me next.

THE GÜIRO

Orchard Beach is so much more than a beach. That half-moon-shaped stretch of sand in the Bronx is holy ground for the Latinx people who go there to party. Sure, the water is a big part of it—you can't swim in the Hudson River and the Bronx River is a toxic waste dump; yeah, there are pools in the city parks where a hundred kids, some of them in diapers, splash around, but if what you want to do is actually swim in the Bronx, the only place to go is Orchard Beach. Once you get out past the toddlers and their shovels, past the splash-taggers, past the bobbers who just like to float in place; once you get past all of them, you can get out to open water and you can swim. There's nothing like that on a sweltering, sticky summer day in the city, gliding through the cool water away from the noise, alone, far from the chaos and the heat. So, sure, the water is why lots of people go to Orchard

Beach. But the vast majority, probably more than ninety percent, go for the party.

The party starts as soon as you drive into the huge parking lot. The air is filled with the sounds of Salsa, Merengue, Cumbia, Hip Hop, and every other possible kind of dance music. The air is also flavored with the smoky scent of barbecue coming from hundreds of portable grills cooking up sauce-soaked ribs, spicy chicken, and all the dishes needed for a summertime picnic feast. So, by the time you've parked and stepped out of the car, you are already in the party space; the questions are, where to set up camp and what adventures will you have.

For me, the music was the thing. Along with the coolers, the colorful beach chairs, and towels, there were congas, bongos, maracas, and güiros. Orchard Beach is packed with percussion, so as you walk around the picnic grounds, and especially near the handball courts, you can hear dozens of jam sessions, with people playing drums, singing, and dancing.

I loved the güiros best because my uncle Pepe always carried one, yes, to Orchard Beach, but also to every single family party. And once he took out his güiro, everyone knew it was time to really get down. The güiro is made from a dried gourd; the insides are scraped out and thin ridges are cut along the top, so that when you run a stick across it, a cool scratchy sound comes out. Play it right and the güiro adds an irresistible magical pulse to the music. A good güiro player was a welcome addition to any jam session, so Uncle Pepe would take me for long walks around Orchard Beach, where he would join up with people whom he didn't know, just start playing the güiro along with them, and they'd let him. It was amazing how strangers just let him into their family hang, right into the middle of their party; without saying a word, he'd be part of the fun. They'd offer us food and drinks, he'd tell jokes, and then we'd move on to another party, and like that for hour after hour; making music, making friends, laughing. Uncle Pepe was the King of the Güiro, and probably the happiest person in our large extended family. And that's what made it so hard for me when Cookie . . .

Well, let me back up. Uncle Pepe and his wife, *Geno* (pronounced Heh-no) had two kids, Sylvia and Cookie. They lived in an actual house in New Jersey, much nicer than our crowded apartment. It was a single-family house, where each kid had their own room, they had a grassy front lawn and a backyard with trees and a swing set, and a two-car garage. Cookie and Sylvia were a few years older than me—Sylvia was already allowed to wear makeup and Cookie had a learner's permit to drive. Everything about their family seemed perfect; the house, the parents, Uncle Pepe's music, how cool the kids were, and, hey, they had their *very own swing set*. Visits to their house were totally fun, and delicious, because Geno was known for her *pernil, platanos*, and flan. So there was fun and food, and when Uncle Pepe took out his güiro, there was music and dancing.

Sylvia knew all the dances, so with hot-red lipstick, mascara, and her swirly skirt, she really got the dance floor going. Cookie loved to dance too. He was really good; he'd dance with everybody, he'd copy everyone's moves, and circulate around the floor so that all of us could take a turn to sharing his joy. But while Sylvia always had a ton of her girlfriends at the house, Cookie never had any friends over. He would hang with Sylvia's girlfriends as if he were one of them. And then he did, he became one of them. I mean, not really, but sort of. Cookie started wearing really over-the-top clothes, like extra-large yellow and orange polka-dot shirts and purple short-shorts, and he grew his hair long, not hippie-frizzy-messy long, more like brush-it-out-for-half-an-hour-in-front-of-the-mirror long. It was weird, but hey, it was Cookie; we loved him no matter what. But Uncle Pepe hated it. The more colorfully

Cookie dressed, the less Pepe laughed, and the less he played the güiro.

Okay, so at Sylvia's eighth-grade graduation party, everyone was there. Sylvia and her girlfriends were dressed in their serious party threads; lots of bows, lots of glitter, lots of makeup. Cookie went to the graduation in one of Tío Pepe's suits, dark blue, with a crisp white shirt and tie. When we got back to the house for the real party, it was decorated with lawn balloons, streamers, and a three-story cake with a little graduation doll on top dressed in a cap and gown. The record player was cranked way up, and the girls started dancing right away.

Cookie disappeared upstairs to his bedroom for a long time, and when he came back down, he was wearing an explosion of rainbow colors; a red and white striped shirt unbuttoned to the middle of his chest, super-tight white jeans, sparkly gold sneakers, no socks, and five blingy necklaces. He'd oiled his hair and parted it straight down the center so that his forehead had these two curly points, and—he had on lipstick. He jumped right into the middle of Sylvia's friends and began to dance like crazy. The girls just went with it, but the grownups stared. To me it was just fun—Cookie was pretending to be a girl, and having a blast at it. Sylvia's friends made a circle around Cookie so he could do a solo dance in the middle; he was spinning, laughing, grinding, and loving having all the attention, when the music suddenly stopped. We all looked at the stereo and saw Uncle Pepe with his güiro.

At first I thought that he was going to start playing so that we could dance to live music, but instead, he lifted the güiro in the air like a caveman's club and came running at Cookie, screaming, "Stop. Go back upstairs and get dressed like a man!" He whacked Cookie so hard on the head with the güiro that blood spurted out all over; it streamed down his face and onto his white pants. Cookie ran upstairs and Pepe chased him. Geno ran behind and so did Sylvia.

I don't know exactly what happened up there, but the yelling and cursing scared me a lot. After a while, three of them came down. Geno was crying, Sylvia was crying, but Uncle Pepe's lips were shut tight and his eyes were bulging, just about popping out of his head. He told everyone to go home.

Their family stayed away for a long time, and when they did start coming around, Cookie wasn't with them, and the güiro never came out. I heard that Cookie moved in with some friends and then fled all the way to San Francisco to live. Uncle Pepe was never the same. He tried to fake it, to pretend he was the same old happy dude; he'd try really hard to make us laugh with corny jokes, but they were as sad as his eyes, and even though he'd play the güiro from time to time, it just wasn't the same. I couldn't understand it, but in some twisted way he preferred to be angry and sad than to accept Cookie for who he was.

I didn't see Cookie for a really long time. It was years. Then, finally, he came back East one Christmas with his boyfriend. His parents wouldn't let them stay at the house in New Jersey, so they camped out for the holidays with us, and it was great. To this day, whenever I hear the sound of a güiro, I remember Uncle Pepe, and the pain that comes from not accepting people for who they are.

PEARL NECKLACE

The way Mom talked about the meaning of life made me think that she really missed Tío Yomo. He'd grown up in a tough seaside town in Spain, made money by diving underwater to pick up sponges, yep, sponges, the *original* sponge, and for most of all history until the invention of factory-made sponges, the *only* sponge, the kind that grows on the bottom of the sea. If you don't believe me, look it up; sponges are a kind of animal. Anyway, Tío Yomo used to put on one of those enormous round brass helmets with a tiny round window, he'd wear weighted boots and a special jumpsuit with an air hose connected to a pump on a boat, and down he'd go with a net, 30, 40, 100 feet, and when he came up, that net would be filled with sponges that were sold all over the world. He would sometimes dive for oysters, the wild kind that grew pearls in the sea, yep, wild oysters, yep, pearls. Nowadays, pearls are human-made; still in oysters, but the oysters live in giant tanks indoors, and only exist to produce pearls, yep, jewels grow in living creatures. All of this sounds like total fantasy, but it's not, it's just the way things are. Tío Yomo stowed away on a freight ship headed for Puerto Rico when he was seventeen. He met my grandpa's sister, Encarnacion; they married and he gave up sponge and pearl diving and went to work in a Ford factory. But those sponges and pearls always were part of our family's story. So of course Mom's meaning of life had to do with pearls, not that she could afford any, but a woman can dream, and she dreamed of pearls.

The idea goes like this: we are each born with a simple necklace around our necks, like a string from a yo-yo, or thin metal wire, or whatever; doesn't matter because it's in your head anyway, and every time we have an amazing experience, a pearl appears on the necklace. Let's say you always wished for a dog and then got one; that would earn a pearl, for sure. Or if you moved to a new school and made an awesome friend, or if you loved someone, but you could only see them once in a rare while; then every time you'd see them, you'd get a pearl on your necklace. Sometimes when I'd see a really old person, I would imagine strings and strings of pearls covering their whole body, and if I saw someone who looked sad, I couldn't imagine any at all.

I think Mom used this pearl necklace idea because of Eduardo too. Eduardo Gonzalez, yep, same last name as me. I think we were super-distant cousins somewhere, like Pluto-distant, but still there was a family link, and still—*Gonzalez?* Eduardo would appear in our lives from time to time, and it was always cool. He had lied about his age and joined the Air Force when he was sixteen, then traveled the world. He knew about electronics; could fix a radio or TV, and owned a fancy camera. Once, he took me to the top of the World Trade Center, yep, the one that was blown up on 9/11. There was an observation deck up there that was a city-block square; you could walk all around it and gaze out over the city so far that you could actually see the curve of the planet. Eduardo showed me that. The earth is round, but how many times do you get to actually see the roundness of it? While we were up there, while everybody was looking way out to the curve of the earth, or down one hundred and ten stories to the street where people looked like ants, Eduardo started taking pictures of people's hands. There were tons of people up there; every color, shape, and age: tourists, kids, moms, dads. Most were holding onto the railing, looking out or down, and Eduardo saw something in their hands he wanted to shoot. There we were at the top of the World Trade Center, and he was snapping pictures of people's hands. It was weird and it was cool; he was different and didn't care what people thought. Later, he told me that you can learn a lot about a person from their hands, the hand tells a story about a person's life. I don't know about you, but I don't have too many other people in my life who take pictures of strangers' hands.

The thing is, they loved each other. Mom and Eduardo had been teenage sweethearts. They had an epic crush—a powerful crush like those places where they take old cars to get turned into junk metal boxes. It was intense. And it was impossible. Eduardo joined the Air Force, and when he came back, Mom was married to my dad. When she divorced Dad and was free, Eduardo was married; when he got divorced, Mom was seriously involved with Alberto, and like that back and forth forever. But that didn't stop them from getting together from time to time. Eduardo would appear at our apartment without warning with flowers and tell stories till late at night, and the stories would continue at breakfast. Mom always looked happy when Eduardo was around; well, mostly; I could also see pain in her because he was bound to disappear again.

Grandma hated Eduardo. And she hated that Mom loved him. And she especially hated when he would sleep over. Talk about *yelling*, talk about *cursing.* Grandma called Mom horrible names and said lots of mean things. She screamed, "How can you bring that man here in front of your son?" I hated Grandma for making Mom so miserable. Mom fought hard for her time with Eduardo, but it wasn't easy.

Eduardo worked as a salesman at a furniture store on 14th Street, where all the cheapo stores were downtown. Sometimes I'd visit him at work. We'd hang out, he'd buy me coffee and a donut, and when a customer came in, I'd sit in one of the gigantic lounge chairs in the showroom and watch him do his thing. I could tell he was fooling the people about the quality of the merchandise, and I could read from his body language that he wasn't into this at all. Eduardo was the coolest, smartest man I knew, so it was hard to see him play this game, and hard to see him see me understanding how this whole show went down.

Once, Eduardo disappeared for a long time, a couple of years, and the next time he popped up, Eduardo was *dressed.* His shoes were shiny ... wait, *alligator?* His shirt was silky and flowery, and he had gold rings on most of his fingers. He had gifts for Mom and me. *Major presents,* like a real pearl necklace for Mom, and a roll of twenty-dollar bills for me, and lots of stories about his business trips to Mexico and Colombia. It didn't take long to figure out that, yep, they were those kinds of trips; yep, that kind of work; yep, that kind of money. And the next time we heard from Eduardo was a couple of years later, in a ten-page handwritten letter on yellow legal paper with the return address of Dade Correctional Institution, Homestead, Florida. Next to his name was an inmate number. Mom was crying as she read it. The tears that fell onto the letter seemed like all the pearls were dropping off her necklace. Eduardo had been caught selling drugs, a lot of drugs, and spent the last years of his life behind bars.

When I was five years old, Tío Yomo bought me my own pineapple from a roadside stand in the mountains of Puerto Rico. He sliced it up with a machete like a ninja warrior and handed me the whole juicy thing. I ate that pineapple, the juice dripping down my face, looking at the mountains of Puerto Rico—that was a pearl.

Eduardo put a whole lot of pearls on Mom's necklace, even though they never had it easy. And even though their story is sad, and even though he messed up really bad, still, the guy with the camera on top of the world slid a whole bunch of pearls on my necklace too.

ACKNOWLEDGEMENT

I want to thank the many people who supported me in writing this book. My son, Jake, was an early reader whose ideas and critique were immensely valuable. Colette Ruoff believed in these stories from the start, her encouragement was vital to the process. My editor/proofreader, Cindy Hochman, polished the texts and helped bring the diamonds out of the rough. Early drafts of these stories were kindly read and critiqued by Tristan C., and other generous young people across the country. A big thanks to my family and friends, you are the ground beneath my feet.

ABOUT THE AUTHOR

David Gonzalez

David Gonzalez received the Lifetime Achievement award from International Performing Arts for Youth, his poetry has been featured at Lincoln Center's Out-of-Doors Festival, the PBS documentary Fooling with Words, and NPR's All Things Considered.   He is the author of numerous theatrical works including: The Boy Who Could Sing Pictures, MytholoJazz, Maddog and Me, Finding North, City of Dreams, Sofrito!, The Man of the House, and Rise for Freedom, which have been presented at performing arts centers, schools, theaters, and festivals across the U.S. David received his doctorate from New York University's School of Education and lives in the Hudson Valley where he enjoys hiking and playing music with friends. www.davidgonzalez.com